Table of contents:

Introduction to the Child's section:	2
Chapter 1: What is Money?	4
Chapter 2: The History of Money	6
Chapter 3: Why We Use Money	9
Chapter 4: How you can earn extra money on top of your allowance	11
Chapter 5: Tips and Tricks for Managing Money	13
Chapter 6: Money Games for Kids Aged 6 to 10	15
Chapter 7: The Effects of Money on Psychology	16
Chapter 8: Ask Your Parents about Money	19
Conclusion:	20
Introduction to the Parent section;	22
Chapter 2: The History of Money	25
Chapter 3: Why We Use Money	27
Chapter 4: Tips and Tricks for Managing Money	29
Chapter 5: Where to start when teaching about money management?	30
Chapter 6: The Risks Of Risk-Taking Behavior	33
Chapter 7: Money And The Ties To Gut-Feelings	35
Chapter 8: The Relationship Of Money To Emotions; Fear, Guilt, Shame And Envy	37
Chapter 9: Games To Help Learn About Money	39
Chapter 10: What Parents Do Wrong When İt Comes To Money Management And Setting Examples!	40
Conclusion:	42

Introduction to the Child's section:

Welcome to "Money Matters," a book designed to teach children aged six to ten about the basics of money, why we use it, and how to manage it. In this book, we aim to demystify money and make it an accessible and engaging topic for children. We will cover the history of money, what it is, and why it's important, as well as share some tips and tricks for managing money, and play some fun games to help reinforce what we learn.

This book is an educational tool that seeks to equip young children with a strong foundation in financial literacy. It provides a comprehensive overview of various topics related to money, including the different forms it takes, how it is used, and why it is important. It explains the history of money, from its early origins as barter systems to the use of coins and paper currency. It also explores the role of banks, interest rates, and inflation, helping children understand the economic system in which they live.

In addition to providing a solid understanding of the basics of money, the book also offers practical advice on how to manage money wisely. It teaches children how to set financial goals, make a budget, and save for the future. The tips and tricks provided in the book will help children make informed decisions about spending and investing, laying the foundation for a lifetime of smart financial choices.

To keep children engaged and help them retain what they learn, the book includes fun games and activities. These interactive elements provide a hands-on learning experience that helps children internalize the concepts they learn and reinforces their understanding of money management.

In conclusion, "Money Matters" is an essential tool for parents and educators who are interested in helping children develop a strong foundation in financial literacy. By providing a comprehensive, accessible, and engaging introduction to money, the book lays the groundwork for a lifetime of informed financial decisions.

Chapter 1: What is Money?

Money is an essential part of our daily lives. It's a tool that people use to buy and sell goods and services. Money makes it easy to trade goods and services without having to barter, which is a system of direct exchange where goods are traded for other goods without using a medium of exchange like money.

In the past, people used items like shells, beads, or cattle as money, but today, most countries use paper money and coins. Money makes it easy to trade goods and services without having to barter, which is a system of direct exchange where goods are traded for other goods without using a medium of exchange like money.

Additionally, money also serves as a store of value, which means it can be saved and used later for future purchases. Different forms of money, such as cash, coins, and bank deposits, have varying levels of liquidity, which refers to how easily and quickly they can be converted into goods or services.

In modern economies, money takes on a more abstract form in the form of digital currency, which can be used to make purchases through electronic means such as debit and credit cards, or through digital wallets. These forms of digital money offer increased convenience and accessibility compared to traditional cash and coins, but they also carry additional security risks, so it's important to understand how to use and protect digital money as well.

Overall, money plays a crucial role in our lives and in the functioning of the economy. By understanding what money is, how it's used, and how it has evolved over time, children can gain a greater appreciation for this important tool and how it impacts their daily lives.

For example, if you have a toy you don't want anymore and your friend has a candy bar they don't want, instead of trying to find something your friend wants that you have, you can just trade your toy for their candy bar using money. This makes buying and selling things much simpler and easier!

Chapter 2: The History of Money

Money has been around for a long time, and it has changed a lot over the years. The concept of money dates back to ancient civilizations, where people used items like shells, beads, or cattle as money. Later, people started using coins made of precious metals like gold and silver. As time went on, governments started printing paper money. Today, most countries use a combination of paper money and coins.

According to the Federal Reserve Bank of Richmond, "The history of money is as old as the history of human society itself. The use of money has allowed people to trade goods and services more easily, increasing trade and commerce and improving the standard of living."

As economies grew and societies became more complex, the use of money also evolved. With the advent of banks, people could deposit their money and use it to make loans to others. This led to the development of paper money, which could be issued by the government and backed by the gold or other precious metals held in reserve by the banks.

However, the use of gold as a backing for paper money had its limitations, as the amount of gold in circulation could not keep pace with the growth of the economy. This led to the development of the modern monetary system, where money is backed by the full faith and credit of the government, rather than by a specific commodity like gold.

As technology has advanced, so has the use of money. Digital currencies and payment systems have emerged, providing new and convenient ways to transfer and store money. The use of digital money has transformed the way people interact with money, making it easier, faster, and more accessible than ever before.

The history of money is a fascinating story of innovation, adaptation, and evolution. By exploring this history, children can gain a deeper understanding of the role money has played in shaping our world and the lives of people throughout time.

Here are a few examples of how money has evolved throughout the centuries:

Ancient civilizations: In ancient times, people used items like shells, beads, or cattle as money. These early forms of money were referred to as commodity money because they had intrinsic value in and of themselves.

Coins: As civilizations developed, people started using coins made of precious metals like gold and silver as money. These coins were more durable and portable than the earlier forms of commodity money, and they became widely used for trade and commerce.

Paper money: In the Middle Ages, people began using paper money in the form of bank notes, which could be traded for gold or other precious metals held in reserve by the banks. This marked a significant shift from commodity money to fiat money, which has value because it is backed by the government.

Digital money: With the advent of the internet and advances in technology, digital currencies and payment systems have emerged. Today, people can use digital wallets to store and transfer money, making it easier and more convenient than ever before.

These are just a few examples of how money has evolved over time. The history of money is a story of innovation and adaptation, as people have sought new and better ways to trade goods and services, store value, and facilitate commerce.

Chapter 3: Why We Use Money

Money is an essential part of our lives, and it's important to understand why we use it. Money is useful because it helps us trade goods and services easily. We can use money to buy what we need, save it for later, or invest it to make more money. When we have money, we have more choices and opportunities.

For example, if you have some money saved, you can use it to buy a toy you've been wanting or to go on a fun trip. Money gives you the power to make choices and purchase things you want or need. As the famous quote by Benjamin Franklin goes, "An investment in knowledge pays the best interest."

Additionally, money is a way to store value. It's much easier to store and transport money than it is to store and transport goods. You can keep your money in a bank account or in a piggy bank, and it will still be there when you need it.

Moreover, money is a means of exchange that allows us to trade goods and services with others. When we trade goods and services using money, both parties are able to benefit. For instance, if you have a skill like cooking and your friend has a skill like gardening, you can use money to trade goods and services. You can cook a meal for your friend in exchange for some fresh produce from their garden.

Finally, money is important for economic growth. When people have money, they can buy more goods and services, which creates demand for products and drives economic growth. Money is also used to fund investment in new businesses, infrastructure, and technology, which contributes to the long-term prosperity of communities and countries.

In conclusion, money plays a crucial role in our lives and in the economy. Understanding the reasons why we use money is an important step in developing good financial habits and making informed decisions about how to use and manage money.

Chapter 4: How you can earn extra money on top of your allowance

Earn money by completing household chores: Encourage children to take on responsibilities around the house and offer a fair wage for their work. Tasks can include cleaning their room, doing dishes, or helping with yard work.

Pet care services: If the family has pets, children can offer pet-sitting or dog-walking services to neighbors.

Sell homemade items: Children can use their creativity to make and sell items such as jewelry, crafts, or baked goods.

Offer a service: Children can offer services such as babysitting, mowing lawns, or washing cars to earn money.

Have a yard sale: Children can gather items they no longer use and sell them at a yard sale.

Encourage children to save a portion of their earnings and discuss the importance of smart money management. These activities can also teach children valuable life skills and help instill a strong work ethic.

Also, children can participate in neighborhood tasks or seasonal jobs such as shoveling snow, raking leaves or helping with gardening. They can also take up freelance work such as tutoring, photography, or graphic design. These opportunities can provide children with real-world experience and help them develop marketable skills.

Encourage children to set financial goals for themselves and work towards achieving them through their earning opportunities. This can help them understand the importance of budgeting and saving.

Remember to always supervise children during these activities to ensure their safety and well-being.

Chapter 5: Tips and Tricks for Managing Money

Now that we understand what money is and why we use it, let's learn how to manage it. Here are some tips and tricks for managing money:

Make a budget: Write down all the money you receive and all the money you spend. This will help you see where your money is going and make smart decisions.

Save money: Put some of your money in a savings account so you can use it later.

Be careful with spending: Think about whether you really need something before you buy it.

Ask for help: If you're having trouble managing your money, ask your parents or a trusted adult for help.

Saving money is important because it helps you prepare for unexpected expenses or future goals. Having some money saved means you'll have a safety net if something unexpected happens, like a family member getting sick or your bike getting a flat tire. Having money saved also allows you to have more freedom and choices in the future. For example, you can save up for a trip or a big purchase you've been wanting to make.

Saving money can also help you build good habits and responsibility with money. When you save money regularly, you learn to prioritize spending and make decisions that benefit your future. Additionally, saving money can help you avoid debt and financial stress, as you have a pool of funds to use in times of need.

In conclusion, saving money is an essential part of managing money effectively. Start small and work your way up to bigger savings goals. The earlier you start saving, the more you'll have in the long run.

Chapter 6: Money Games for Kids Aged 6 to 10

Here are some fun games that will help you learn about money:

Age 6: "Money Match" – Match different coins to their corresponding values.

Age 7: "Spend and Save" – Play pretend store and practice making purchases and saving money.

Age 8: "Budgeting Bingo" – Fill out a bingo card with items you might need to buy, and practice making a budget.

Age 9: "Investment Adventure" – Pretend to invest money in different scenarios and see how it grows over time.

Age 10: "Allowance Challenge" – Set a budget and track your expenses for a week, trying to stick to your budget and save money.

Here is where you would ask your parents for some guidance to set up the games.

Chapter 7: The Effects of Money on Psychology

Money plays a big role in our lives and can have a big impact on our psychology. Understanding the effects of money on our thoughts and feelings can help us make better decisions and lead a happier life.

Positive effects of money:
Money can provide a sense of security and stability. When we have enough money to cover our needs, we feel less stressed and more relaxed.

Money can give us freedom and independence. It allows us to make choices and pursue our passions without worrying about financial constraints.

Money can bring joy and happiness. When we are able to buy things we want or experience new things, it can bring us a sense of pleasure and happiness.

Negative effects of money:
Money can create stress and anxiety. When we don't have enough money to cover our needs, it can lead to feelings of fear and worry.

Money can cause conflict in relationships. Disputes about money are one of the leading causes of relationship problems.

Money can lead to materialism and a focus on possessions. When we place too much value on money and material possessions, it can take away from other aspects of life that bring us happiness and fulfillment.

It's important to remember that money is just a tool. It's up to us to use it in a way that brings us joy and fulfillment. By understanding the effects of money on our psychology, we can make better decisions and lead a more balanced life.

Negative role models can greatly impact our perception of money and how we handle it. Whether it's a family member, friend, or public figure, the actions of those around us can greatly influence our beliefs and behaviors when it comes to money.

For example, if a role model consistently spends beyond their means, it may lead us to believe that it's acceptable to live beyond our means and constantly accumulate debt. This can lead to poor spending habits and a lack of understanding of the value of money.

On the other hand, if a role model prioritizes saving and smart financial decisions, it can inspire us to make similar choices in our own lives. This can help establish healthy financial habits and a strong sense of financial literacy.

It's important to be mindful of the individuals who shape our perception of money, and strive to surround ourselves with positive role models who embody the financial principles we wish to emulate. By doing so, we can develop a positive relationship with money and make smart financial decisions that will benefit us in the long run.

Sources:

"Money and Happiness: A Guide to Living the Good Life" by Elizabeth Dunn and Michael Norton (2011)

"The Psychology of Money: How Our Finances Affect Our Emotions and Behaviors" by Brad Klontz, Ted Klontz, and Rick Kahler (2017)

"The High Price of Materialism" by Tim Kasser (2002)

Chapter 8: Ask Your Parents about Money

Your parents are an important resource for learning about money. They can help you understand how they budget their finances and make smart choices about money. Here are some things you can ask your parents about:

How do you make a budget?
How do you save money?
What do you do if you need to buy something expensive?
How do you invest your money to make more?

By talking to your parents and learning from their experiences, you can become a savvy money manager and make smart choices about your finances.

Conclusion:

Congratulations! You now have a good understanding of what money is, why we use it, and how to manage it. Remember, managing money is a lifelong skill that will help you make smart choices and reach your goals. Keep practicing and have fun!

Additional :

Here are some additional resources for parents to help answer any questions your child may have about money:

Encourage them to ask questions: Encourage your child to ask questions and talk about money. This will help them feel more comfortable with the topic and grow their understanding.

Lead by example: Children learn by watching what you do. Show your child how to make smart money choices by making them yourself.

Teach the value of earning money: Teach your child the value of earning money by giving them a small allowance or having them do chores around the house.

Visit a bank: Take your child to a local bank and let them see how money is saved and used. You can also teach them about interest and how savings accounts work.
Discuss big purchases: When you make big purchases, like a car or a home, explain to your child why it's

important to save up and make smart financial decisions.

Have fun: Money can be a serious topic, but it's important to have fun with it too. Play the games and activities in this book with your child and make learning about money a fun and interactive experience.

I hope this book is helpful for children in learning about money management in a fun and engaging way. Enjoy!

Introduction to the Parent section;

As a parent, it is important to guide your children towards a healthy and responsible relationship with money. This guide is designed to help you teach your children about money management, setting and sticking to a budget, saving for the future, and making smart financial decisions. By establishing these habits early on, you can help your children develop a strong foundation for their financial future. Whether you are just starting to teach your children about money, or looking to reinforce what they have already learned, this guide is a valuable resource to have.

In this guide, you will find practical tips, activities, and games to help your children understand the importance of managing money wisely. You will also learn how to help your children develop positive money habits, and how to avoid common mistakes that parents make when it comes to money management. The guide covers a range of topics, including the basics of budgeting, saving, investing, and debt management. By following the guidelines in this guide, you can help your children build a strong foundation for their financial future, and ensure they have the tools they need to make informed financial decisions.

Chapter 1: What is Money?

Explain that money is a form of currency used to buy goods and services.
Show examples of different forms of money, such as coins and bills, and explain how they are used.

Talk about how money has changed throughout history, from bartering to using coins and now using digital currency.

It's important for parents to educate their children about money and the role it plays in their lives. Money management skills are essential for a successful and financially secure future. In this guide, we will cover the basics of money and help parents explain it to their children.

In addition to explaining what money is and its different forms, it's important to emphasize the value of saving. Encourage children to save a portion of their allowance or gifts to build a nest egg for future purchases or investments. Explain that having savings can provide financial stability and the ability to handle unexpected expenses or emergencies.

It's also important to talk about budgeting and making smart spending decisions. Teach children to prioritize their spending and make conscious choices about where their money goes. Emphasize the importance of avoiding debt and living within their means.

Finally, discuss the role of money in achieving personal goals, such as saving for college, a car, or a down payment on a house. Showing children the power of money and how it can help them reach their aspirations will foster good money management habits that will last a lifetime.

Chapter 2: The History of Money

Explain to your children how money has been a fundamental aspect of human society for centuries and its evolution has allowed for increased trade and commerce, improving the standard of living.

Discuss how ancient civilizations used items like shells, beads, or cattle as a medium of exchange. Then, how the use of coins made of precious metals like gold and silver became widespread and eventually, paper money was introduced by governments.

Talk about the recent developments in technology and digitalization, which have led to the widespread use of digital currency, such as credit and debit cards, online banking, and digital wallets.

Emphasize how money has always adapted to changing times and its importance in allowing individuals and societies to exchange goods and services more easily and efficiently.

Highlight how this evolution of money has contributed to the growth and development of economies and societies throughout history. Also, emphasize the role of governments and central banks in controlling the money supply, issuing currency, and regulating financial systems.

Point out the advantages and disadvantages of different forms of money and how they have impacted individuals and society. For example, paper money and coins can be easily lost or damaged, while digital currency offers greater security and convenience but also raises concerns about privacy and the risk of hacking.

Finally, stress the importance of learning about the history of money and its evolution, as it provides valuable insights into how money works and how it affects our daily lives. Encourage your child to continue to educate themselves about money, finance, and economics to help them make informed decisions about managing their money in the future.

Chapter 3: Why We Use Money

Explain that money is used as a means of exchange for goods and services.

Discuss how money helps us to compare the value of different goods and services and make decisions about what to buy.

Talk about how money is used to save and invest for the future.

Emphasize the importance of having money to make choices and purchase things we want or need. Discuss the benefits of saving and investing, such as being able to buy larger items or achieve financial goals, such as retirement. Explain the concept of compound interest and how saving and investing early can have a significant impact on future financial stability.

Mention how money also serves as a store of value, allowing individuals to save for emergencies or unexpected expenses. Stress the importance of setting financial goals and creating a budget to ensure proper money management.

Use real-life examples and scenarios to help children understand the practical uses and importance of money in our daily lives. Encourage children to think about how they can use their money to make positive choices and impact their own financial future.

Additionally, educate children on the consequences of irresponsible spending and the impact it can have on their financial future. Explain how impulse purchases, such as buying something on a whim, can lead to debt and negatively impact financial stability.

Teach children about the difference between wants and needs, and encourage them to prioritize spending on necessities, such as food and housing, before non-essential items. Show them how to make informed decisions about spending by weighing the costs and benefits of each purchase.

Moreover, highlight the role of money in the larger economy, such as how it helps businesses grow and provides jobs for people. Explain how taxes and other financial obligations, such as paying bills and loans, are necessary for the functioning of society and maintaining financial stability.

By teaching children about the history, uses, and importance of money, they will have a foundation for making informed and responsible financial decisions in the future.

Chapter 4: Tips and Tricks for Managing Money

Mention how creating a savings plan, such as putting aside a portion of each paycheck or allowance into a savings account, can help build a safety net for unexpected expenses or emergencies.

Emphasize the value of smart spending and avoiding impulse purchases. Encourage children to consider the cost-benefit of each purchase and think about whether it is a necessary expense or a want.

Teach children about the importance of being a responsible and informed consumer, such as comparing prices and shopping around for the best deals.

Share strategies for reducing expenses, such as using coupons or cutting unnecessary subscriptions, and explain how these small changes can have a big impact on overall financial health.

Encourage children to take an active role in their financial education and provide resources, such as books or websites, to help them learn more about money management.

Chapter 5: Where to start when teaching about money management?

To teach children about healthy money management with the help of reward circuitry, it is important to understand the way rewards influence behavior. The reward circuitry in the brain releases chemicals, such as dopamine, which create a feeling of pleasure and motivation.

Here are some tips to help children develop positive money management habits through the use of reward circuitry:

- Set achievable goals: When children set achievable goals and meet them, the reward circuitry in their brain is activated, creating a positive association with smart money management.

- Celebrate successes: Celebrating financial successes, such as reaching a savings goal, can reinforce positive money habits by activating the reward circuitry.

- Offer small rewards: Offering small rewards, such as a treat or extra allowance, for good money management habits can encourage children to continue making smart financial decisions.

- Make money management fun: Children are more likely to engage in activities that they enjoy, so try to make budgeting, saving, and investing fun for them.

- Use visual aids: Visual aids, such as charts or graphs, can help children see the progress they are making and activate the reward circuitry in the brain.

By utilizing the reward circuitry in the brain, children can develop positive money management habits that will benefit them in the long-term.

Additionally, teaching children about delayed gratification and the benefits of saving for future goals can also help activate the reward circuitry. Explain how waiting for the reward, such as a big purchase, can increase the sense of accomplishment and satisfaction once the goal is achieved. This can help children understand the importance of saving and budgeting, and create a positive association with smart financial decisions.

Incorporating games and activities that focus on money management can also be an effective way to engage children and activate the reward circuitry. These activities can help reinforce the concepts learned and make money management more interactive and enjoyable for children.

It is important to regularly check in with children and discuss their progress towards their financial goals. Offer support and encouragement, and celebrate their successes to further activate the reward circuitry. With these techniques, children can develop a positive relationship with money and make healthy financial decisions throughout their lives.

Chapter 6: The Risks Of Risk-Taking Behavior

Risk-taking behavior can have a significant impact on an individual's financial decisions and money management. Risk-taking is defined as the willingness to take on uncertain or potentially negative outcomes in exchange for potential rewards. When it comes to money, risk-taking behavior can lead to impulsive spending, investing in high-risk financial products, or taking out loans with high-interest rates.

On the one hand, taking calculated risks can lead to financial growth and increased wealth. However, excessive risk-taking behavior can result in financial losses and lead to debt and financial instability.

The level of risk-taking behavior is influenced by a variety of factors, including an individual's personality, age, cultural background, and past experiences. It is important for individuals, especially children, to learn about the consequences of risk-taking behavior and how to make informed financial decisions.

Parents play a crucial role in shaping their children's risk-taking behavior when it comes to money. By teaching children about budgeting, saving, and smart financial decision making, they can learn to make informed choices and avoid excessive risk-taking behavior.

In conclusion, risk-taking behavior has a significant impact on money management and financial stability. It is important to understand the consequences of risk-taking and to make informed financial decisions. By teaching children about smart money management habits, parents can help them develop a strong foundation for their financial future.

Chapter 7: Money And The Ties To Gut-Feelings

Money and the ties to gut feelings refer to the unconscious emotional and psychological responses people have when making financial decisions. Research has shown that emotions play a big role in how people handle their finances, and that many financial decisions are made based on instinct rather than rational thinking.

For example, when faced with an investment opportunity, people may rely on their gut feelings to make a decision, rather than thoroughly researching and analyzing the potential risks and rewards. This can lead to impulsive or irrational financial decisions, which may result in financial losses.

Additionally, people's emotional responses to money are often tied to their childhood experiences and cultural background, which can influence their attitudes and beliefs about money. For example, individuals who grew up in a family where money was a constant source of stress and conflict may be more likely to experience anxiety or fear when making financial decisions.

It is important for individuals to understand the role that emotions play in their financial decisions and to work towards developing a healthy relationship with money. This can include seeking professional financial advice, educating oneself on personal finance, and practicing mindfulness and self-reflection to better understand one's emotions and motivations when it comes to money.

Chapter 8: The Relationship Of Money To Emotions; Fear, Guilt, Shame And Envy

Money has a complex relationship with a range of emotions, including fear, guilt, shame, and envy. Understanding this relationship can be key to making healthy financial decisions and avoiding negative financial outcomes.

Fear of financial insecurity is a common feeling when it comes to money. People may fear running out of money or not being able to pay their bills, leading to anxiety and stress. This can result in making impulsive financial decisions or avoiding money-related activities altogether.

Guilt can also play a role in financial decisions. People may feel guilty about spending money on themselves, leading to a lack of self-care and an inability to fully enjoy their hard-earned money. Similarly, shame can be a factor when it comes to debt or financial hardship, leading to feelings of inadequacy and a fear of judgment from others.

Shame can cause individuals to avoid financial discussions or hide their financial struggles, leading to unhealthy financial habits. On the other hand, guilt can drive individuals to overspend in an attempt to make up for past financial mistakes. Recognizing the impact of these emotions on financial behavior is important for developing a healthy relationship with money.

Envy can also be tied to money. People may compare their financial situation to others, leading to feelings of inadequacy or resentment. This can result in making impulsive financial decisions in an attempt to "keep up" with others, or feeling discouraged and disengaging from money-related activities altogether.

It is important to recognize and address these emotions when it comes to money. This can involve seeking professional help, such as financial counseling or therapy, or working to reframe negative thoughts and beliefs about money. By understanding the relationship of money to fear, guilt, shame, and envy, people can take steps towards a healthier and more positive relationship with their finances.

Chapter 9: Games To Help Learn About Money

Additionally, use the games as an opportunity to reinforce the importance of budgeting, saving, and investing. Also, highlight the value of making smart choices with money and avoiding overspending.

Encourage children to practice counting money and making changes with the games, helping to develop their math skills.

Incorporate discussions about the different forms of money, such as coins and bills, and how they are used in the real world.

Use the games as a way to have fun while learning about money and to create a positive and engaging learning experience for children. Additionally, these games can also be a great way to start conversations with children about the importance of good money management and to build a foundation of financial literacy.

Involve children in conversations and ask their opinion and what they would do in this situation. You might surprise yourself on how they approach problems and how creative their ideas might be.

Chapter 10: What Parents Do Wrong When İt Comes To Money Management And Setting Examples!

When it comes to money management and setting examples for children, there are several common mistakes that parents make. Here are some to be aware of:

Not talking about money: Talking about money with children helps them understand the value and importance of money and how to use it effectively. When children are aware of the financial decisions made by their parents, they can learn about budgeting, saving, and investing. This education can help them make informed financial decisions in their own lives.

Overindulging: Overindulging children can lead to a sense of entitlement and a lack of understanding of the value of money. When children are not taught to save and make smart financial decisions, they may struggle with money management as adults.

Ignoring their own financial problems: Parents serve as role models for their children, and their financial habits can have a significant impact on their children's attitudes and behaviors towards money. If parents ignore their own financial problems, their children may learn to do the same, leading to unhealthy financial habits and difficulties in the future.

Failing to set a budget: Setting a budget is an essential part of financial planning and helps individuals prioritize expenses, save money, and avoid overspending. Without a budget, children may not understand the importance of saving and may develop unhealthy spending habits.

Not teaching children about debt: Understanding debt and the consequences of overspending is an important part of financial education. If children are not taught about debt, they may accumulate debt without understanding the impact it can have on their financial stability and future. By teaching children about debt, parents can help them make informed financial decisions and avoid financial difficulties in the future.

It is important for parents to be mindful of these mistakes and strive to set a positive example for their children when it comes to money management. This will help children develop healthy financial habits that will benefit them in the long-term.

Conclusion:

Point out the significance of developing good money management habits from a young age and how it can positively impact their financial future. Emphasize that money management is a lifelong skill and it is never too early to start learning.

Discuss the benefits of being informed about money and making smart financial decisions, such as being able to afford the things they want, avoiding debt, and reaching financial goals.

Encourage children to be curious and ask questions about money and how it works. Remind them that they have the power to make a positive impact on their financial future through informed decision-making and responsible money management.

Finally, encourage children to apply what they have learned to their daily lives and make it a habit to regularly review and evaluate their financial habits.